LEGACIES

For Ann + Richard
+ Fiona

Leanne E. Began
January 1997
Ma

Also by Suzanne E. Berger

These Rooms, Penmaen Press

LEGACIES

Suzanne E. Berger

Book and Cover Design by Susan Graham
Typeset by Ruth Goodman
This book is set in New Baskerville.

Printed in the United States of America

The publication of this book was made possible with
support from the Massachusetts Council on the Arts and
Humanities, a state Agency whose funds are recommended
by the Governor and appropriated by the State Legislature.

Library of Congress Catalogue Card Number 84-070353
ISBN: Hard Cover   0–914086–48–0
         Paperback   0–914086–49–9

Alice James Books are published by the Alice James Poetry
Cooperative, Inc.

Alice James Books
138 Mt. Auburn Street
Cambridge, Massachusetts 02138

ACKNOWLEDGMENTS

Grateful acknowledgment is made to the following publications in which some of these poems first appeared.

Agni Magazine: "In the Evening of Creatures"

Aspen Anthology: "The Grievers," "Lady"

Harvard Magazine: "The Promise"

The Massachusetts Review: "The Sister-Fish"

Ploughshares: "Over Chicago"

Prairie Schooner: "Light"

Tendril Magazine: "Myth," "The Meal," "Parts"

"Adam Naming the Creatures" won the *Duncan Lawrie Prize* in Sotheby's International Poetry Contest, and it will be printed in the anthology of contest winners.

With special thanks to the MacDowell Colony, The Virginia Center for the Arts, and the Ossabaw Foundation, where I had the privilege to write some of these poems.

And with gratitude to the members of the poetry group, close and far, and to my parents.

For Michael and, now, for Zoe

CONTENTS

In the Morning Dark

After Knowledge

Destinations

In the Morning Dark

LIGHT

Came the rain-light,
spattered over the earth's raw marrow:
then hot light came, untrapped
from the fire's loose sweet core.
Came the stealthy zig-zag gaze
of cats and lizards,
animal eye-light poised
for the prey, the milk,
the gizzards of others.

Came light, first motive
for the shiny buds
of infant eyes to open.
Then exotic light came seeping
like the tropics, such red and yellow,
under parents' closed doors:
then a whole churn of light,
like cream; came longing,
compressed light held in,
a pulse between thighs.

Birds came,
becoming wing-light,
traveling over winter sparseness:
light, we inhale it, we drink it,
it fits like a membrane around trees,
and through the hands, such prisms.
Came, this morning, light like a scalpel
to open deceit, our perfect-skinned apple:
how close to the surface its ripe meat lay.

ADAM NAMING THE CREATURES

My tongue, the new spade to dig through
the acres of namelessness,
Genesis' lush and dreaming mud.
In exhalation, there will be names.
In logos, dominion and order.
Word-skins to fit the creatures
in the cacophony of spinning dark:

You will be *Snail, I am who I carry,*
I am who I shield, with tentacles quivering
in sleep on the Hiddekel's oozing banks.
And you, the sister called *Turtle*,
who wears a leathery sadness,
whose labor rocks out a glisten of eggs,
small moons for these first nights.

And *Fox*, his fur burnished by hot wind,
he lies down, flashing blue-white tendons,
his teeth a snare for the grape and the meat.
He broods over a rookery
of feather-sticks, who are *Birds*,
the grass of prehistory in their claws.

Birds, with wings that flash through the sky,
do you weave air out of yourselves,
or does the air extrude you
to this wildest, speckled firmament?
Free, free, free, you clatter:
Who looks at you shall be moved with flight.

And *Bear*, ursus, the brown-gummed dreamer
eating up his own fat
in the stinking chamber of winter sleep:
he who consumes himself, yet lives,
who wakes up with hunger smeared
on his dripping jaws.

And I, frail bone shaking in this new world,
I live by my syllables and vowels
that, rising, ricochet through
the glare of palmettos.
With the fat and protein of these words,
I increase myself, attaching names
like second carapaces, shells and fins.
The cosmos thrums, beating with the noise
of flying and crouching,
their hissing and climbing.

You will be *Bats*, flutter-mice,
with greasy sails on finger-bones,
whose upside down sleep
invades ours like an incubus,
innocents with defiled and defiling faces.
Fly quietly past *Giraffe*
of the long blue tongue,
past *Walrus*, who walks on her own tusks.

And *Whale*, out there on the seething waters,
with mound shaped like desire,
who bleeds grey to color the ocean,
whose bright saliva is the waves' crest:
contralto, warbler in the longest miles
of opera, muted under fathoms.

And how shall I describe
the creature of coiled knowledge
that crept into me
on its diamond-studded back?
Through time, I shall bruise its head,
and it shall bruise my heel.

And you I call *Beaver, I am teeth that grow forever*,
who must always gnaw to trim them down—
or mouths blocked, die in streams, unable to eat.
Pity such a killing growth
that would starve by its own vigor.

Poised near the streams are *Deer*,
evanescents, with eyes
the very cups of trembling,
whose tails glow like new clouds,
as they graze on ferns rooting deep
in the shock of this rising sun.

And you, tainted black pig of the world,
understand that we—
the tribe of sky-searching,
upward-walking shafts of flesh—
we will never love you.
You must drag across the world,
this sty of pain,
by your own haunches, your own dumb bulk,
past pitch and tar and slime,
while we lurch above you,
spectators of the animal chaos,
and all that is animal within—
while we watch you rut and bask and lie
in the green carbon forest,
denying that the shine of grime
in your scarred eyes
is the grimy light in ours:
Oh son, misbegotten, oh daughter, ours.

MYTH

There was a sky that wanted to be man:
being sky, it had to bend a little down,
to flatten. There was a river

that wanted to be woman, to be liquid
in a different way from water. One day,
they met, creating each other's first bones,

new flesh. They shouted, *We are powerful*,
as they tore love out of the rosy air.
But this substance was stronger

than they expected, like holding
a swarm of flaming bees.
There was a battle, until battle

grabbed the love away: they had never
imagined the after-color of rampage.
Astounded, they stood in one place,

while white moss grew over them
like one long skin. Only their eyes poked out.
All night they eyed each other,

unblinking, until they saw what they had done.
In a tightening circle around them were worn-out trophies,
distance, lies. So, with an endless magic,

she turned him into a sky, which darkened
to a hole black with anger. And magically,
he transformed her into a river,

endlessly filled with salt,
with the sounds of a raspy choking.
And where they moved, or rained, or flowed,

the foliage charred, the animals broke,
men and women lay down in the odor of disenchantment.

.

IN FLORENCE

I

Below the Piazzale Michelangelo,
the city churns out a sepia light.
City whose separate children we are,
we grow naked and what strips us
later leaves to hide
in blue steam exhaled by the hills.

II

Outside the hotel window,
rooftops move away jaggedly.
I turn to you, I am always entering
the perspective of you
which vanishes as I approach.
Over hot terra cotta tiles,
the multiple bells of Florence
beget each other, generation on generation,
thick with dolor and bronze.
Sacrilege is crouched in the corner,
a desire to believe in the God
who is the tongue for the bells,
and to make love while believing,
arched in the large music that is belief—
so that our flesh, and the limbs of faith,
couple and fix us in a moving fresco.
If only music could heal, be an unguent between us.

III

Decay on green marble, soot in striations,
over the Duomo's dizzying whites—
beast of time on whose rounded back
pilgrims have ridden silently
toward an endless dream of God.

A child asks, "If I break the wafer, will it bleed?"
Adults explain the skeins of transubstantiation.
In the hundred Florentine churches
prayers are groaning from the faithful,
nuns search for the Bone of Him,
for the cherubim's substantial wings.
In one reliquary, a frail finger-joint
studded with a crustacea of pearls,
and St. Agnes' shank tied with white ribbons,
obscenely iridescent through the centuries.
Perhaps, those who believe find more to see, to taste:
their eyes full of ornate icon,
their tongues sated with wafers.
Our eyes have a lens that reduces and empties,
our tongues taste each other, are not resplendent.
Is there a chamber in this city
where even the unbelievers can press
their salty palms together and call *Jesu, Jesu*,
calling him like an old dog
to walk at their fraying sides?

IV

In the morning dark of Masaccio's world,
Adam and Eve are fleeing across the fresco.
Her face, the contorted deer's
stunned at night by the hunter's lamp,
his head bowed like a boy's,
hands covering his eyes
which are the exact shade of grief.
Though they could comfort each other,
they do not touch . . .
Before, an innocence blind as a root,
and a singular breathing between the creator
and the shadow-fabrics of his self.

Then knowledge came like a scythe, and separateness,
moving between them—
to her, *I will greatly multiply*
thy sorrow and thy conception.
To him, *cursed is the ground for thy sake,*
in sorrow thou shalt eat of it.
Expelled from the garden of ourselves,
can I ever enter you,
or you uncover a luminous place in me?
In sorrow, in multiplying curses,
they will till and labor;
we will grope through a lamentation of light.

V

On the terrace, a dusk exotic as a new language,
and cream-white magnolias
pulsing like votive candles.
At the blue fountain, a mongrel drinks
the water's brown stench.
The madonna of light is streaming
her dark gold over these streets,
flocked with pilgrims and agnostics,
aged children of remorse, hosanna.
We go into the city, and everywhere
is the Duomo, the dreamless beast whose shape
we meet around each corner,
repeating like marble shadows of ourselves
we can never lose, or leave behind.

THE FANATIC, SPEAKING FROM
THE ASYLUM

*According to the sand dollar legend, the openings in
the shell represent the nail holes and spear wounds of
Christ. Inside are small shells, "the doves of peace,"
and on the top, an outline of the Easter lily.*

Broke it, I had to.
They told me stigmata would grow on me,
I'd catch them on the wood of my hands and arms.
Held it up, the sand dollar, and counted the holes,
which are wounds which are windows.
The birds inside, are they really angels made of bone?
I am a root, but they can fly.
The angels fall down in the sand like ash.
Which of the wounds is the spear wound?
This flower, is it a lily, does it burn?
The holes in myself which are windows.
They told me the lily would grow into a spear
and then pierce me . . .
The wounds, they are windows, do you hear me?

This shell is a frail house,
it took millions of years to build.
Nothing built me . . .
Sometimes they call it the *Holy Ghost shell.*
If I ate it, I could be thin as a ghost.
Isn't this a wafer, this is a wafer I know it.
Have I burned and broken the house
of the angels which are birds?

The sky it poured through me, through the holes
and down into me, I drank it, the sun got too close.
I needed to break the wafer, I needed to taste
the salt of the angels inside.
I only broke it, I didn't burn.
The holes in myself which are windows,
forgive me.

THE BLIND MASSEUSE

I am washing them in touch.
The sinewy warmth of back and thighs
is like a heating stream,
muscles beneath the surface
like hungry fish, wanting to break through.

Sometimes I am so parched
I want to drown in steamy depths,
to let myself go under, flailing.
But skin, skin is the sun that burns me
with a silken punishment—
I rub in sacrament.

> *All flesh is grass, Isaiah said.*
> *Then I am like the wind,*
> *moving its fingers over and over.*

Their bellies are lean with barrenness,
their buttocks curve with gleaming fat.
I smooth in hot clove oil,
that spatters near my eyes—
these vestigial blanks.
Fragrant scalp is tantalizing as musk,
and hair is flax in a winter field
or soft, the tiny whips of rain;
all hair feels like fur stretched out,
then hammered fine, fine.

> *Oh Christ, I sometimes say,*
> *though I am no believer,*
> *Hammer me to sight.*

I make the sharp animals in their nerves flee—
when I touch their necks, I pull
against the muscle-feel of anger
drawn like leather pulled too tight.
Pressing on the temple's veins,
I am so near the brain
my hands are the voyeur
at the windowed circuitry of thought.

> *Is that what vision is?*
> *Circuits that electrify and glow,*
> *to fill the empty shape of color,*
> *give voltage to the felt edge?*

When they leave, I know what absence looks like—
a coldness that scrapes
and tempts me toward a different blindness—
a deeper kind of grey.

> *Gone, the rough and silky braille*
> *of their flesh.*

Tomorrow brings new supplicants,
spines and twisted tendons,
the heated undulations of the skin.
And bodies that, breathing, sound to me
as light would sound
if light could breathe
before it is extinguished
in the storms of darkness
always breaking through these eyes.

FAILURE OF ABSTRACTS

        Flakes of stone
are falling, falling from the sky.
Stone woman, sour leave-taker,
I feel dark today as soot,
the sooty earth you fled,
riding a white horse to Kingdom Come.

Where is Kingdom Come?
I asked in the glistening church
that shimmered like a white mirage.
Children have always stood
in pews and at the rainy graves,
biting their fingernails:
Where did you go? Where's the tobacco smoke?
After the starving children die,
where do they go?

How far is heaven from home?
And when it was raining cats and dogs,
I thought that yapping and meows
would fall from the substantial clouds,
mongrels, angels of fur winging down.

        The abstract fails
and falls away from me in pieces,
death the meat of absence
our minds would try to eat.

Though I know cellular return,
the detonating journey of body—
stone man, ash woman, dirt of dust
that breaks to sky and rains back down,
blown compost of toes, fingerprints—
the ecology of *gone*.
This knowledge I leave behind
like a broken toy.

Tangled in the ice of inquiry,
I stand over the ditch
of the anniversary of your death,
speaking to the deaf white that is *Not-heaven*,
where the lost are not, not ever,
and I grow backward
to the child-shaped questions:

Where are you? Why don't you take up space?
If I count to a million in eights,
will you return? If I say it
with stones in my mouth,
to make it harder . . .

       And the snow
continues to dream downwards,
speaking to emptiness,
cold language falling
through a blue cipher.

COATS

This morning, I dreamed of you
calling back to me,
you were standing there
hesitant as sparrow, and pale,
an arctic air bristling
the down on your arms:
Please bring me some coats.
God makes it so cold here.

So I brought you a blue coat,
the color gravity would be,
to bring you back here,
earth-bound and safe.
Then I offered a silk coat,
with silk wings
and a fur hood against all the ice.

In the speed of the dream
I wove a coat
from the thread of my hair.
Then I found the old ermine coat
you wore to costume parties:
no one knew then
your costumes wore you
in their huge dark sleeves.

Finally, I bought bolts
of precious cloth, gleaming like opals,
and fashioned a width
for your bird-thin shoulders,
though I knew I could not change any weather—
with my gravity, bribes, and jewels.
Though I still run to you now
like a kite in the wind of the dream.

After Knowledge

COMING BACK

*I fear those shadows most that start from
my own feet . . .*

Theodore Roethke

I

Too large, too dark and alive with flaming shadows,
this house I built like a blind carpenter,
house always tilting off in a wrong wind.
Terra infirma, terra dolorosa.
Cracks of the house, splinters inching in,
years brought to their knees . . .
I built that house, stubborn house;
I made the earth unfirm, I made the axis swerve.

> *Was she really useless except for lying down
> in the sepulchre of herself?*
>
> *She never remembered. Blackout, blackness,
> did she really run into that car? Did she really
> fall down on the ice that night? Someone who
> must have been her fell down, absent from time.*
>
> *What bird of oblivion was drinking her up?*
>
> *As she drank, the bird drank, camaraderie
> on snowy nights, in foul spring, in summer-torn
> nights, in the fall.*

The moon drinks up the black of urban roofs:
out pours clarity, its unbearable shine.

II

The moon is a slice of white melon above the bed
in a room with one window, flies moving
over the moon like black pieces of extinguished stars.
Behind the moon is crazy weather, the self's lunar heat.
A confusion of elements, moon and sun spinning
together, autumn chill in summer, blades of snow,
a bleeding shine of spring moving in winter like a knife.
Whatever season I was in, the lost and the dead
kept swimming up through the green pools
of their long transit, rippling to the surface
with unwieldy strokes—
coming to visit, the sometime-swimmers. . . .

Those days, a small beauty would waken me
from self-pity and torpor: stubborn marigolds,
the cat's snuggle, warm as a glove on the hand.
I wished she could take the craziness
and lap it up like milk, could lead me out
from where I lay, where my mouth was a speaking cave.

> *Where was the Borden's country girl,*
> *the ad for butter and cream?*
>
> *She fell down, she was as lost to herself*
> *as meat on a rack in an icehouse.*

III

The mind is the real stomach of the body,
scavenger eating the past—the past the food that starves.
You grown thin as razors, thinking you are cutting
the air as you move through. But famished,
you make no impression. You think an acid liquid
will dissolve razor-thoughts in a cold room.

34

What you want is revelation, under the Bo-Tree
in the Buddha legend—only it is the Bourbon-Tree
you lie under, you are lying to . . .

IV

Bleary-eyed at a chic party, breaking all
the rules of decorum, as a dog muddies a room,
I ask some strangers: Do you love me? I love you.
Do you really love me?

> *Why did she embarrass herself that way?*
>
> *She was a free sideshow, sweating in the July heat,*
> *presenting the rags of herself to sell*
> *for the small currency of strangers' affection.*

It was an especially good show that night.
I remember it well.

V

The oil of the woman is fading to watercolor:
the stark eyes run down in a pastel wash to the mouth,
her pose is collapsing, her limbs dangle and splay
on icy streets and at gatherings of other shadows.

At last will be invisibility, the frame dissolved.
Or perhaps she will use the canvas of herself
as a butcher's apron, or as floor covering—
the way the invaders used Pissarro's paintings
for animals' defecation.

Like a doctor, I speak to her who has become an invalid
in the portrait: *Get up, do anything, eat.*
Be a janitor at the zoo, be anything, but at least get up.

But the invalid prefers the half-life
of her house with its dank familiar odors,
and the magnetic field of dark that draws no one in,
prefers the stained and steel-wool hours,
the days like white holes into which everything disappears.

Blackout, whiteout, time has occurred,
but she's not in it, dumb as a smudge on a canvas.
For there is no invisibility.
The watercolor woman just walks out to more ice.

VI

Dear X, You say to starve the demons out, don't water
them any more, so to speak . . . To stay away from them.
They're bad bed partners and worse drinking buddies.
Here's a question for you: Rilke said, If they take
away my demons will my angels disappear too? I know
what you'll say, something like—which would you rather
have? Angels on vacation, or demons in your house for good?
But I'm afraid my angels will disappear and they're all
I have now. (I know you'd call that self-pity too) I am
toasting them now. *Love, me*

Propellers of dark are churning: walk toward them,
do not weave, enter their quick wind.
Lorca's horses are on the roof, with hoofs of pain;

or are they God's Horses? Anything is better than being
awake like this, coming back from shadows
to a glaring portrait that disappears in daylight.

VII

Notes from the animal world, another house:
the tiger sleeps on top of its kill.
The lioness will feed herself first
even if the cubs are so thin
the wind shines through them.
Beached whales die, crushed by their own weight.

She sleeps on top of herself in a hotel
where each room is a lost intention,
each door a promise that slams closed.
The jungle moves in, a lullaby of predation,
tropic fevers, black leaves and nexus.

Outside in Chicago, a monsoon roars,
she is in Africa, Iowa, Dubrovnik.
The small nude voices of the self recline
in a ditch in Indonesia, they want to be buried
in Rome or in India: *O bury me in excrement.*
they sing. *I am too pitiful and of a caste too low
for cloth, gold shroud, or even dirt or shovel.*

Thus the carpenter extends the house, over and over,
the same house of monotonous leaping dark.
This is the house with deadly walls and floors,
creaking and sighing, a house containing
imaginary weapons, teeth and claws.

VIII

Nights, with three sheets to the wind,
or wherever sheets and bottles go, I'd pucker up
for one good suckle on the phone, for the words
of father-doctor, dream-divining rod, healer of tribal woes:
Teach me, I slur. *Who built this house?*
Tuck me in, take care of me. Who did this?

You, he answers all the time. *You did it.*
Not me. Not me, I baby-talk, *but grief.*
You, he repeats, the urban witch doctor.
Get some sleep.

I would lullaby myself to sleep, drunk and sour,
curling into bed obedient as a puppy,
dumb and full of sloppy love.

IX

The dark and debris of the house, the shadows
had begun to fall into the corners of the real body.
The angel of survival, of comfort went looking
for a beautiful meal of new perception.
Next to her, I stood uneasily—is she my sister?

We look at the house that grief built;
it begins to burn. What was it,
that black throne for counting the losses
carefully, every day, like dark money . . . ?
A one room for the bleak furniture of the nerves.

The body began to push away and eat, blessing.
Forgive us our trespasses against ourselves,
lead us out . . .

X

Sometimes the nude wires of clarity
exposed themselves in the mirror of morning:
how the desire to murder the losses
can get dressed up in the desire for self-kill
and go walking through the halls,
and how dread is the real poison
that will not flush out of the body.

Led out, and leaving the house she built,
there she stands, the self-made weeper, crying dust,
grieving for what she herself had done,
watching the house begin to fall.

XI

All the women in my tribe have fluttered like moths
to the weeping light of asylums.
They are kites sneaking from the low altitude
of their lives into closed hot rooms,
wearing thorazine inside like perfume,
and blue slippers in the halls.
I have always visited them with aphorisms,
brownies, yellow roses that have their thorns
removed by nurses—the flower as dangerous tool.

All flesh is grass, Isaiah said.
And perhaps it *is* better to be grass
inside these hothouses,
covered in hot mother-light,
in the dirt of surrogate fathers,
with nurses gentle as gardeners
and doctors pruning into desirable shapes.

Not me, not me, I said, wobbling away
from hospitals on the way home
for more oblivion—but becoming free.

XII

Dear X, When you remind me of those years
I hate you. Maybe you didn't think I'd make
it through, but I knew. Dear friend, in fact
the dearest, let's forget all of it, though I can remember
for both of us the day when I called,
helpless with real hunger, sprawling:
Can you bring me some food, a piece of fruit,
some cheese? Of course I love you, but when you
mention all of this, your words are like a plate
I want to smash. So anyway, don't remind me.
It makes me feel like some dog on an old leash. *Love, me*

XIII

After the last room's burning,
and the doors are scattered to particles,
the burning vanishing house
still tilts in the wrong wind.
But all flesh is grass and grows like grass, indomitable.
It was a strong house,
stubborn with joists and beams.

Naked as grass, as full of dumb green will,
I walk away, steady, shadow on steady shadow.

In the distance, the vanished house shines, and burns.

for Polly Bennell and Michael Wisneski

EARLY MORNING AT THE YWCA

The flowing meadow
of water, skin,
skin and water:
the mind grazes
in a doze,
the breasts pearl
with steam—Yes,

it is possible
to forget everything,
to have boundaries mix out
like milk in water.
The city has not yet begun
its dissonant toil.
Like minnows, water swims

through our mouths,
heat rises against
long pool windows.
Outsiders who want to
look in
are turned away.
Hair in rivulets, streaming,
we kick and unfurl,
coaxing each shy muscle—
Yes, it is possible

to open and join,
desiring only ourselves,
flowing like estuaries
in the early hush.

WHITE FOG/DESIRES

I

White fog blurs
these spiked Virginia trees
to a Japanese serenity.
The cows are steady in desire,
browsing through the snow-grass,
scratching on barbed wire.
Their hides tear there,
and hang like pieces
of brown winter sky
caught on the spokes of stars.
Cows, tomorrow's dumb meat:
why do they love what takes
their propitiary skins away?

The wire, a slash
against the blue-white mountains,
washed in watercolor.
Walking close,
the human dare is to touch,
to sharply feel—
the hungering toward hazard.

II

The whole landscape limned in white,
a dusty fog.
You can hardly see yourself, or want to—
outlines are lost, seeping into white.
Obscured by fog that drifts, then lifts,
the blurred wire seems to move closer,
away, then in again.
Further white now, hungry for more of itself,
deep white dark:
Fear can read by any light.

III

Fog has been drinking
the black leaf-wire of trees,
soaking them in white so completely
that background, foreground disappear,
a white removal of perspective and desire,
except the always famished greed—
to see, to blend, to lose yourself and not to.
How far is that barn?
How close the wire that scratches steady near the mind,
a steady numbing out?

I need my self, we need the selves
we want to lose and fear—
to be together
serene as figures
in an old landscape
who watch the cows go up,
the cows graze delicately down
in winter search of winter's stingy protein.

IV

Warm, shoulder to steaming shoulder,
the cows are divided now:
some to milking, some to slaughter.
In the red and lunar white
are the colors of all our transits.
Imagine there is more than this.

Imagine the wire, and other dares,
not there.
A large enough pretending
can paint in soft black strokes
a silent truce,
a peaceful self-to-self deception,
sealed in white.

In the white blood of fog,
the cows look up
from dumb brimming lakes of eyes,
as though already drowned in red,
and tranquil.

V

Later, the fog is a white rag
that soaks up the noise
of the slaughter barns
where mute blurry worlds are lost,
and soaks up the low crooning music
of milk-givers
in their daze of falling milk.

What is possible?
Something stark and quiet—
to start down a shadowy field
in mute descent,
avoiding the wire
like teeth that gnaw invisibly
at the meat of inner landscape . . .
to start down in a delicate trance,
telling lies, making truces
to appease the steady hungers.

THE PROMISE

For those afraid of the dark
and its empty sleeves,
there is a place lit by animal-comfort—
to hold against the skin,
fur to the naked pelt of ourselves

Listen, whole families speak there,
the geodes of their words, glowing:
There will be waking,
there will be enough bread

And taste the rain there:
It harvests a repair people dream of
Its crops shine with the after-taste
of sun and morning

Enter, look closely, lean towards
this far place,
somewhere its bright seeds scattered
in the planet of the body

Destinations

THE MEAL

They have washed their faces until they are pale,
their homework is beautifully complete.
They wait for the adults to lean towards each other.
The hands of the children are oval
and smooth as pine-nuts.

The girls have braided and rebraided their hair,
and tied ribbons without a single mistake.
The boy has put away his coin collection.
They are waiting for the mother to straighten her lipstick,
and for the father to speak.

They gather around the table, carefully
as constellations waiting to be named.
Their minds shift and ready, like dunes.
It is so quiet, all waiting stars and dunes.

Their forks move across their plates without scraping,
they wait for the milk and the gravy
at the table with its forgotten spices.
They are waiting for a happiness to lift their eyes,
like sudden light flaring in the trees outside.

The white miles of the meal continue,
the figures still travel across a screen:
the father carving the Sunday roast,
her mouth uneven as a torn hibiscus,
their braids still gleaming in the silence.

THE SISTER-FISH

The aquarium in the house
has sisters swimming in it.
Food glitters on the surface like snow.

The gnarl of coral entices them.
They have always mistaken the thin plants
for lifelines, swimming between slabs of glass.

The temperature is constant,
the pump is a fist which clenches, unclenches the water.

The little one tucks her gills, and searches
for a grotto, lips opening and closing.
Then she sucks again on a stone.

The other begins a comfort—
the phrases break off in the water.

For a while they swim together.
They are the only historians of these waters.

The little one is becoming transparent,
like a scaleless fish whose bones can be seen,
whose organs are tiny swells of color:

as though diving and searching
rubs the flesh down to a surface of windows,
where spectators can gaze.

They have chosen this, moving in a caul of water.
The seasons quietly slide through the box.
Sometimes sounds can be heard:

> *Oh little-fish, I'd put fat*
> *on the clear needles of your spine*
> *I'd bear you away if I could*

In the aquarium in the house,
all things dissolve, like sugar, when spoken.

AFTER CHOPIN

In the pearl-colored early hours,
they are playing Chopin
before the melancholy adults
are awake.
She plays by listening,
a lean moth lifted on Chopin's rounded air.
He plucks the over-ripe notes
from the keyboard
and smoothly they both are hammered
between the levitating silvers
of etudes and ballades,
the excessively sweet mazurkas.
Chopin, Chopin, they repeat,
swelling the *O* to contain—
what was it?
Does music stretch by over-filling,
like desire?

Figures turning at clarity's edge,
children of unremitting August,
keep this, drink it.
This was longing and the young end of it
a widening to keep music in—
music to break through
the closed octaves of solitude,
beyond any later myth of night,
beyond any crescendo, decrescendo
played on the imperfect lengthening ivory
of the days, and of the body.

Where is it, that scintilla of noise?
No one can keep it.
Begin again, *lento*, in mute rooms,
on the staffs perished by older weather:
music that floated
to the listening lake outside
while the others slept unhearing,
unblessed through their dreams,
and the children played in hours
that left an after-music,
a bruise of longing, after Chopin.

for Bruce Berger

WAITING

I

Spring still kisses
its false promises at the window,
and cigarette smoke is drifting
like greyish weather
through the waiting room.

This is the hour of nerves,
in this Ohio hospital.
A scalpel glints,
and the low moon of the breast
is taken, the body's luminous cloth, torn.

The air keeps gleaming on outside
like Renoir's green euphoric weather
where mother and children live in high pastels
dazzled with leaves and a rapture of health;
the pretty ingenuous lies
of the mothers perfectly curved as pears,
of children who always wear roses for skin.

II

Quiet as steam, nurses are moving
through our portrait on rubber soles.
Anesthesia lifts, my mother looks out
from under its hood
to the truth
of curtains drawn around the bed,

of the hidden new concavity,
of inches of blood flickering through tubes
like slowed insects.
The jello trembles in the shaking spoon I lift—
the child who feeds the parent
feels younger than any child.

In this too bright clarity
of afternoon weather,
we wait . . .
what will we hear next,
what next will we know?

FOUR GIRLS IN A RED ROOM

(after a painting by John Singer Sargent)

The patrician faces of the girls
bloom and glow like magnolias
in the still reds of the room.
Shining boots are painted on feet so fragile
they barely attach to the canvas.
Someone invisible is calling
from a far corner of the scene.

In the translucent dust of the museum,
air wanders over them like a second brush.
This is a lie of perpetual afternoon,
a place of white silk stockings
where the contemplative children
are always full of memory and tea,
and never darken for each other.
A long Afghan hound lounges near them.

Hesitantly they begin to move,
trailing velvet dresses,
losing their petals and perfect silks.
They step out into a dark blue weather,
leaving the words of the beseeching someone.
Red, the interior—
pigment of flowing stasis,
of desire to enclose and keep—
the red will always be.

WE

G. and F. are identical twins in England who talk in unison, speaking the same words. They were arrested for breach of the peace after constant harassment of a man on whom they had developed a fixation . . .

from *The Boston Globe*

We are one peat fire for two
rooms, a single tongue of speaking.
In York, the ragged crones and filthy children

pelt us with garbage and stinking hay. We are not
a witch: do they think that with their pebbles
and tomatoes they can make us walk apart,
push us to the separate sides of the street?
A stone flung on the pond does not divide
the water. In autumn, when the fog

is a thick cold pudding, we
close the door against the rainy damp,
and the other, larger cold: the cold of all
those strangers who live in the cold tatters
of their separate bodies . . . How poor,
just as it must be to eat a piece of suet alone
on a dreary Monday morning—

one plate with one fork warms us. Every morning, we
wake and part the curtains, to watch him
wash and eat—fried toast and eggs,
and how he dresses in those cheap and drafty wools.
Our hand could make a better scarf, but he refuses,
refusal always. How can he leave us,
each day lurching away in that banged-up truck,

when we need him like butter, money, meat?
To make him less alone, less full of cold tatters
and rags, we warm him with our watching. We
stop at his pub, and sit across the smoky room from him.
When he is drinking his ale, we want
to be the ale. When he plays his whist, we
are the darts, the shiny tips, the aim,
the target. But he is always leaving . . .

A year or so ago, a rainy early morning, we
got dressed and went to him, taking our umbrella.
We stood in front of the truck, we
wanted him not to leave, to be close as our shawl,
our second set of arms under our rough blanket.
To stop him was so simple—we lay down
in front of the tires, our umbrella lay beside us.
For that the Magistrates came, and called it

breach of the peace, and said that we were guilty.
We had to move away, but now we're back
near him across the street. And the way we
see it, the longest breach is really this:
most of the world is a dank potter's field,
with the harsh wind blowing over. We never
wanted him to be like that, not

a separate stone in the sharp weeds.
When he has a stone, we will lie beside, we
will be his warming twin, peat for three
rooms in a final colder winter.

HEXES

I

I am surrounded by diaries, a drift of ten years,
torn-out pages settling around the room.
I must read their illegible rage,
the young color of their grief.
The hushed tent of my life is open again.

In the morning there are more words,
an over-abundance that stains the day.
My hands have written them,
moving like quiet gloves through the pages.

II

Toe by toe, I step into a pool of love.
I have never known such heat, such clarity.
We are touching like fish, shimmering, nibbling the sun.
All we can imagine are raspberries, bourbon, milk, jazz,
and our thighs touch, our hands,
the tangled silk of our voices.
Your hand is a wing, our bodies are like warmed plums.

You leave, and I dream of another pool in a snowy country,
where other loves and all fathers weep
from looking, too deeply, into the ice.

The pool turns suddenly to brine.
I must stand by the pool, sip from it, and eat their tears,
a double-salt in the overexposure of snow and dream.

III

It is so beautiful, the day with snow rolling
over its own hulk in the forest.
I believe in the steady peace of snow,
I have always believed I would enter this quiet.
The cabin is warm, the fire is dark red and excessive.
I could sleep in such beauty,
the solitude like a glass fence around me.
I am no longer a cut, longing to open further.
Even the fox loves me, as he eats orange peel in the garbage.

I look outside, and yes, there are cardinals,
imaginary snow-fish, snow-cats and lizards.
The high windows constrict and focus,
and I see what was and what will be—
their torn shapes—
hung like forgotten rags between the pines.
My words travel out there,
to greet that huge memory of me,
tangled in the white expanse.

IV

I am with my father and talk spools out.
The wires of each other have finally connected.
Standing on the boathouse roof,
we will fish for blue gills in the lake, again,
on the white lake in Wisconsin.
In the transforming light, the pole I have is silver,
the blue gills are endless, the day is endless.
The fish-line winds out.

Suddenly, snow surrounds my father, pours down
on the roof where we stand.
He slips, he hangs there, he is fluttering.
His sleeves are what I have known of warmth.
I am frozen, I am an ice-child
who must stare at the movie of blue gills and fathers.
My arms grow heavy with unforgiving snow.

V

I am on a beach, I am acquainted with no one.
Hibiscus flowers fall over me, deep pink confetti, streaming.
I am lying in my skin like a good hammock.
I am resting,
The brown lizards graze over my body.
I am happy, I desire everything.

I turn in the lap of the sand,
its confusing, powerful heat, and I see my name,
written in tar, a hex of letters
in this place I have never been before.
The sand turns to snow, it gathers like a white membrane
around the final syllables of my name.

LADY

Here in the hot suburban grove,
we wheel our old ones
who slump like ragdolls in their chairs—
away from the bone-cry,
the belly-cries that hide
in the expensive nursing home.

All afternoon, you've wanted
these blighted crabapples
to be a shining orchard,
you've told me grandmothers' secrets:
Do you believe it? Twenty-five years,
and he never told me he loved me.
Do you want some vanilla pudding?
You are a bud of slow nerves,
perched on a body stalk.

And I will be you, and not-you;
time cat-claws down your cheeks.
Does God punish me, to make me live so long?
Queen of disdain, age and the drooling others
are beneath you: you stiffen parchment shoulders.
Promise me I'll make it to next year.
Then you grow back to my age,
haughty at the parlor's edge,
gathering skirts for flight.

Just off the grove, the traffic
drags through the heavy net
of a heat wave; your clouding eyes
retreat from the glare of chrome.
You reach up again, almost like a child,
and again the crabapples prick your fingers:
Where are we, Lake Placid? Is Chuck still alive?

For you, I will remember
when green was warm and lush,
despite the steel hands of a husband,
when you wore a flowing chiffon
and not the lonely rag pulled
from a confusing pile this morning.
Now, I roll you back, sleeping
in your spider-legged stroller,
and I center you where you can watch
the grove glisten, then recede—
if you want to look, *liebe*, if you want.

OVER CHICAGO

Generation gone to fragments,
atomized grandmother, recluse,
I am above Chicago for the last time,
meeting you outside the window,
still alone in your lonely particles,
a drift of shattered lace and body.

I fly through your rising dust,
cutting through like a scythe,
above you and with you.

And now we are flying together,
you in your white boat
sliding through time,
in your pink shawl still redolent
with stale Chanel . . .
We are drinking the finest Darjeeling tea
though I always wanted gin.
You are playing bridge,
and the scattered aces and spades
rise and disintegrate in the altitude.
You play your last hand, dealt fast
with faceless cards in the dark.
I play mine, shaking in the half-light
of hotels and airplanes.

We are flying together, you and I.
But where will we ever land
on this eating earth
that spits the no-color ash of us
back to the blank blue air?

THE GRIEVERS

We had tried to send them away—
to forget the set blue knots
of their mouths,
to put out, like a harsh lamp,
the memory of their empty breath.

Now, like color, the grievers are brushing
against our eyelids,
renewing the warmth they have lost,
murmuring again
they have missed us,
that their grieving need for us
fills them like a new pulse:
how, from what they remember,
dying is a twisting away,
a traveling without miles.

Our desire to assuage them
is very great, like a reflex—
too swift to control.
Some days, we need to find them,
to reach for the braille of their palms,
and we want to follow, to close
the long raw seam between us.

POSSIBILITY

Through the tough ice
of January,
I drive toward you—
a second growth for me,

closely held and shining.
In the white dusk
the headlights blur—
suddenly, a crushed heap
of cat on the road,
the only cut of color:

Don't kill it a second time.
I brake and skid,
unmoored in the currents
of wind and snow.
Adrenalin heats my blood,
then leaves me breathless
at the jolt,
the abrupt shift—

lush fur
turned to broken stain,
mud to lethal ruts in winter.
All of it, in seconds,
in seasons,
swerving layers
of a world
that is accident

that is a geology
of distress.
Ready as a knife,
the edge lives with us,
the possibility
of exposed bone and nerves—
metal, love, gravel
flying out

over the curve,
the guard-rail
bending like a lie.
And you, waiting,
imagine wreckage
incandescent

as the yellow-gleaming
eyes of a cat
as it crosses the road
without motive
in the sharp white dusk.

RESCUE ATTEMPT

Again the enemies are digging trenches
through your sleep, cutting you with the dream.
Their S.S. caps grow from their heads
as naturally as the beaks of birds.

You sweat, you roll over, you resist
a lieutenant who offers you poison soup.
Troops walk through the yellow snow of the room,
clutching grenades like bags of jewels.
Soldiers are using our sheets for pup tents.

Stretched to you like a life-line,
I want to use my body as antidote,
its smoothness to bandage whatever is tearing.
I want to smother the armies, to warm your hands,
freezing at prayer in a fox-hole.

You wake up, you're crying and shouting again,
then you grind your fists into the pillow,
while the enemies wade through a swamp
beside our bed, holding their guns up,
never once dreaming of truce.

PARTS

In the room
boundaries are torn away
in layers like gauze,
and then—
letting go—
wounded places are exposed
and the salt air heals,
stings open
like love, again

Then silence
moves like a thick light
in the room
where a woman kisses
the knees of a man,
where he is threading her
through a needle of desire,
and part of her
is the wasp on the sill,
part the thread,
and part the shine
on the needle, flickering
Flickering like the ocean,
which offers its beauty, its hunger—
I need you, I need you—
which offers the possibility
of drowning.

IN THE EVENING OF CREATURES

Exuding the nude odor of time,
    the humpback heads ram up,
        freckled with chalky barnacles.
            Wake up, I'm afraid.
    Crusted whale-eyes swivel from the bleached sky
    of Genesis to the oblivion
        behind oblivion.

When they make love, genitals hidden,
    is it missionary style?
        One ton a gleaming shelf
            for the other gleam of ton to lie on,
    a double-weight sorrowfully heaving
        from an earlier world . . .
    Or up in the air, perpendicular columns locking,
    whale-flesh sculpted from whale marble?
            What would whales think about? you asked.
            The failure of humankind to sing,
            the will to make ourselves extinct.
Grazing through the cold meadow
    of galactic swimming,
        whales whistle, moan and grunt,
            noise torn from the black noise of prehistory.
        resurrected, spouting.

Beached, their huge pounds of brightwork suffocate;
    from the shore, incredulous humans watch,
        the human brain their lethal weight.
    On the sinking sand
        each whale flipper is the progenitive shadow
        of finger-bones in your hand that pulls me
    swimming up from sleep to the bruised crest
        of the day.
            If it happens, we couldn't
            reach each other.

Close as your pores, distant as lunar pull,
　　　something in the magnetic pull of the sea
　　　　needs us to thrash back primordial,
　　　　　using our lost dorsals, spilling ambergris,
　　　　spouting the half-truths
　　　　　　of human love.
　　Afterwards, stillness holds its breath,
　　　we even sing a little,
　　a smoothness drifts above us,
　　　　　like the smooth slicks the whale flukes leave,
　　　slapping on the water.

We do this, mirroring all
　　with our humid mammal embrace,
　　　　　the drinking up of salty other . . .
　　In this, a moving barrier of flesh, skin to skin,
　　　we stave off what we know
　　　　of the future extinct,
　　　　　　of eons burning like paper,
　　of creatures all un-creatured.

And do others turn as we do,
　　trembling less with love
　　　than with a chill underwater prescience
　　saying, *Hold me.*
　　　　　There won't be time.

POETRY FROM ALICE JAMES BOOKS

Thirsty Day   Kathleen Aguero
In The Mother Tongue   Catherine Anderson
Personal Effects   Becker, Minton, Zuckerman
Backtalk   Robin Becker
Legacies   Suzanne E. Berger
Afterwards   Patricia Cumming
Riding with the Fireworks   Ann Darr
ThreeSome Poems   Dobbs, Gensler, Knies
33   Marjorie Fletcher
US: Women   Marjorie Fletcher
No One Took a Country from Me   Jacqueline Frank
Natural Affinities   Erica Funkhouser
Without Roof   Kinereth Gensler
Bonfire   Celia Gilbert
Permanent Wave   Miriam Goodman
Signal::Noise   Miriam Goodman
Raw Honey   Marie Harris
Making the House Fall Down   Beatrice Hawley
The Old Chore   John Hildebidle
Impossible Dreams   Pati Hill
From Room to Room   Jane Kenyon
Streets after Rain   Elizabeth Knies
Dreaming in Color   Ruth Lepson
Falling Off the Roof   Karen Lindsay
Temper   Margo Lockwood
Shrunken Planets   Robert Louthan
The Common Life   David McKain
Animals   Alice Mattison
Openers   Nina Nyhart
Wolf Moon   Jean Pedrick
Pride and Splendor   Jean Pedrick
The Hardness Scale   Joyce Peseroff
Curses   Lee Rudolph
The Country Changes   Lee Rudolph
Box Poems   Willa Schneberg
Against That Time   Ron Schreiber
Moving to a New Place   Ron Schreiber
Contending with the Dark   Jeffrey Schwartz
Changing Faces   Betsy Sholl
Appalachian Winter   Betsy Sholl
From This Distance   Susan Snively
Deception Pass   Sue Standing
The Trans-Siberian Railway   Cornelia Veenendaal
Green Shaded Lamps   Cornelia Veenendaal
Old Sheets   Larkin Warren
Tamsen Donner: a woman's journey   Ruth Whitman
Permanent Address   Ruth Whitman